Gog

Gog

Brandi George

Black
Lawrence
Press

Black
Lawrence
Press

www.blacklawrence.com

Executive Editor: Diane Goettel
Book and cover design: Amy Freels

Copyright © 2015 Brandi George
ISBN: 978-1-62557-926-3

Published 2015 by Black Lawrence Press.
Printed in the United States.

Excerpt from "Eleven Addresses to the Lord" from COLLECTED POEMS: 1937–1971 by John Berryman. Copyright © 1989 by Kate Donahue Berryman. Reprinted by permission of Farrar, Straus and Giroux, LLC.

for Michael

CONTENTS

I. PRETTY BANSHEE

TO OVID, MICHIGAN

Cow-mother, I counted all the one-eyed cats
in town. Grandma said I'd go blind.
Did you see me on the graves? I was born dead,
took my fifth of vodka to the cemetery.
Did you hear me praying? I said
there was no god, so who was I talking to?
I've seen ghosts with no teeth, and I want
to escape inside their mouths.
Ovid, I'm naked almost all the time now
inside my boxy apartment. Remember
I pressed my breasts to your dirt?

CRONE-BALLAD

When my great-grandma's husband drove by with another woman,
 she punched him in the face.
When her daughter married a rapist,
 she punched him in the face.
When her son slept with her other son's wife, then slid
his motorcycle under a semi truck,
 she wore a red dress to his wake.

There were blue birds, red birds, gray birds whose tails salt
 wouldn't bind. There were great-great-grandmas, aunts, uncles,
 peering through glass.

When her husband kicked her pregnant belly,
 she earthed the stillborn in a shoebox.
When the bruises spread like violets,
 she earthed the stillborn in a shoebox.
After she named her Sharon Rose and dug an unmarked grave,
 she washed the livings' socks.

A loosed canary flies into the glass.

When her husband left his first family in Hungary, the woman
 cursed his children to die young.
The woman he left in Hungary
 cursed his children to die young.
In a tiny town in Michigan,
 her boys dropped one by one.

Birds line up on the sill to peck the glass.

*

Great-grandma said:
Forty years of pot roasts, hams—
my lingerie hangs
in the closet, still tagged.

Each time we saw their stitched faces,
        we passed the opiates,
        flicked cigarettes into a vase.

In her dream, she told me:
                It was red.
It was the red scarf.
It was the red scarf around the neck of
the pregnant girl
he left in Hungary.

*

Great-grandma spits into her garden,
complains about a treaty her Blackfoot mother signed.
She hates crops. She hates farmers.
I stomp a colony of ants.

We practice
        shooting cans. I shave my legs
with her purple razor. The wildflowers
        bloom all at once.

Even in winter, I pump my legs
on the swing set, cold turning my chest
to a porcelain egg
where my great-grandma's stillborn
scratches and turns.

There is one way to escape the dream: break your neck against the glass.

*

The last words of Mary Warren Toth Seibert Prochaska:

Lousy cocksuckers.

She approaches death
like a wounded bear. Her red-tinted
hair heralds her combustion; her
heart is packed with gunpowder, and she'll drag
us down with her. Goddamn.
Every breath is a supernova, a blue
membrane sparking around her shadow's
husk. She's a triple-shift, three-husbands-
before-1960, tarot-reading, play-any-instrument-by-ear,
ham-fisted, ammonia-in-the-bathwater,
pick-your-teeth-up-off-the-floor bitch.

MOTHER IS A WOLF

She says *Yes* is a woman's word—
        a rubber ball that doesn't fit
      between her teeth—the baddest wolves
      wear masks. I pass the time attaching flies
to strings and stringing pupils into wreaths
of irises. O lightning, fangs! Old crones
      wear shoes worth more than us,

    and I am wild. Mother strikes "chicken"
    from the dwindling grocery list.
  Her fists and feet scrape bone
into whole pies. I fetch
      empty chip bags from the unmowed
    perimeter of our trailer. Spam bursts
    from my abdomen. I demand
  car alarms. I force
bug zappers to outshine stars. I will collapse
      the brick house. I will loose
  myself far and wide as pink light
on a field, and emerge—Mother—
      my own child, For Whom
    Branches Bend to Touch.

    Mother, emaciated by another miscarriage,
  limps the hospital halls, convinced
the rape that scarred her
      was earned; she growls
    weak into my ear. I roll myself in clouds,
    six, seven, eight. I have been

the shadow and light of each year,
each star folding itself into a nipple
            caked with blood, but that is how we feed
        the ones we love, without a sound and when we can.

Danielle, Penelope, Joshua, Sharon: sleep.
  I'll paint you grown and in every
        color, write you songs in A minor, sad
and easy for your mouths
like string-less lyres outside my window.

HOMUNCULUS

I couldn't stand silent while my father cocked his rifle
at each thing small enough for him to own. I was a boy

who turned into a girl who was called a liar
by everyone I loved. My spirit in that angular, wiry form

was winged and bloody like a fang. A sparrow,
cardinal, and starling lined up on my father's windowsill

and pecked the glass together: snare, timpani, bass.
I've become the wolf, the bastard son who dove

off a cliff into shallow water. O tiny changeling embryo,
self-sculpting clay, you are a pecking mass in the shadow

of a bolt-gashed tree, a dreamonym for dust.

MEADOWS TRAILER PARK, 1995

We scribbled fake police reports,
asking Jenny to circle in red
the places where her father touched her,
then dialed 911 from payphones, snickering
at the cops while we hid behind bushes,
collecting rocks to hurl at people
too weak to chase after us. Then
your little brother died,
his lips and eyes glued shut in the coffin because
he ate rat poison, and we should have
watched him better. You breathed
from that milk jug bong until
the universe was the sparrow
you had tattooed on your shoulder blade.
When our mothers were crushed
by their father's desire for them, we lit
our hair on fire. I want to tell your mom, I
spilled the chocolate milk, give you back
the honey blonde ponytail she hacked off,
let you taste my magic egg soup, admit
that I was afraid of the deer's eyes, too.
And when you washed the horse manure
from my shoes, I would keep quiet.
I would keep quiet when the other Brandy
from school said her mom had sex
for money, that one day
while she was watching cartoons,
her mom and some guy fell
naked through the second story floorboards.

HER MOUTH, A STRING-LESS LYRE

At East Street Cemetery, I find a grave that fits
    the recent curve of my chest, wait for the cosmos
to line up with my spine, worms struggling
      toward the newly created universe
 of my thighs, my body still giving birth
to more cells than it loses. I call her
    my sister, my love,

        make my ribs a cradle
for her to sleep in, her umbilical cord hooked to the earth.

I tear her free, and we play hide and seek
in the pillared mausoleum. Danielle, born dead,
 draws her name in cursive loops,
      beholds the lowest frequency
of a rainbow, cuts off my fingers, takes them
        as her sacrifice, each second
    my body creating more blood, more cells,
    so we can begin again. Snakes spin the world

in reverse, and I see Mother hanging clothes
 on the line, her canned tomatoes, tan skin, uncut
    abdomen, two shining fallopian tubes, and the tiny
zygote, cells dividing. Pretty banshee—unbinding.

MOTHER'S RED WEDDING DRESS

Wouldn't fit me. *Big boned*, she said,
Grandma could knock a man out.

That year, I put a kid's head through a window.
Blackout rage, damaged film

in my retina. I'd been in another's mouth
who kissed, ate ice cream, then spit

on my cheek. *Don't talk about my mother.*
My spine split and healed jagged

as a saw blade, mouth grew to a snout.
Get that dress away. I'll lick the meat

from your ribs like that dog
we threw food—gone wild from chains.

DANIEL STANDS AT THE GATE OF THE KING

the WWII vet   at my grandmother's nursing home
dreams of the German girl he raped   the king
of an idol's iron feet   Daniel predicts
my mother's at fifteen   Daniel   name dragged
through history   soldier's name   unborn son
she would miscarry   the radius of a circle
to the brother who was aborted before me   four
great beasts   originating from the uterus
four future kings   Daniel dreams the dead
sea scrolls   I used to think   engraved
on his spine   I was a boy   all my life
old vet   pouring milk for cats   suet for finches
I dreamt   minutes   seconds   was a soldier
cutting his wrists   in a hotel sink

SUNDAY TRACTOR PULL

Mother bites her lip, still
glossed from early morning service,
and shifts gears, while old men
watch the weight inch up
the transfer sled. Her long braid
unravels like sparks of wheat
they'll part each sunrise, squinting east
and east through fields. I'm reading
Sweet Valley Twins and wishing
I were Jessica, while the world watches
my mother dismount
from a 1938 Allis-Chalmers.
She's a primal sky gazelle,
a shovelful of black soil
like what sticks to our knees
after pulling thistles. We snap
string beans. We bristle
the earth from our fingernails.
We're made of Gerald's boot,
billows from the track, matchbox
Thunderbirds. Old men's beers
spray diamonds, ball caps tip
in praise. The forest-combed air snaps
a promise: Death is a bright green vine.
As the sun honeys fields
around us, we find ourselves
in the silence between
engine pops, spit from a calf's
conched mouth. The metal bleachers

burn our thighs, so my mother drapes her flannel
beneath me. And eagles weave
golden nests from her wind-born hairs.
I don't tape my breasts.
Father doesn't hunch all afternoon
making ammo. He pays his taxes.
When my mother miscarries and almost dies,
he agrees to adopt a son
and names him Joshua. Mother finishes first.
And she's Queen of Red Flannel Days,
her tractor-shaped trophies
gild the mantle. She doesn't walk;
she's carried, and everything
she touches sings. I don't pluck
the buds off her azaleas. I don't wander
mint fields alone. In this story,
after the first frost kills the tomatoes,
there are two puffs of breath
in the yard—mine, my sister's.

ELEGY FOR MYSELF AT SIX

I found Katie the year I forgot
how to blink. In the flowerbed,
she wandered among the poppies—
        a tiny calico.

I had become an absence
 of laughter, last year's child
cold in my mother's belly.
            She'd hired a boy to burn
                    ditch weeds, I remember
            the ache of breaking skin
            like scorched earth; my eyes
                burned as I held
            a kitten's starved body to my face,
            marveled at her leafy irises,

        but that summer, I couldn't stop
        brushing my hair, flattening my hair,
        stealing my mother's makeup,
scrubbing my skin raw, then Katie
        and I lay on blankets, inches
from each other's eyes, fighting sleep.

                So a few years later, when I found her
            in a field—long-decayed, bits of orange
                fur clinging to exposed bone,
                    a single bumblebee emerging

from her eye socket—I harbored a fire
without kindling, the lost six-year-old
pinned at the joints, the way a shovel
splits hard ground.

FOR EVA, WHO I AM NOT

Alone, my great-grandma passes
      a stillborn girl, arranges the limbs
inside a shoebox. Hours later,
            she snaps the neck of a chicken
         and makes dumplings for the living three.

Five decades later, I jump
      off the garage roof, don't even break
my legs. At night, I sleep on graves
            to prove how sad I am,
         how close to death,

while her fingers shake
      too hard to play piano. I sing
"The Old Rugged Cross" to her, and she begins
            calling me Eva, her mother's name,
         the name my mother had almost given me.

And when she refuses food, tries to yank
      out her feeding tube and rasps *let go*, I refuse.

II. RED BIRD

LOVE MANIFESTO

Because of the iris' yellow tongue, the bouquet
        my father picked from the creek bed
    his giant leap over water,

I plant each bulb.

Because in a storm trees sound like infants, the arrowheads
    I gather from the forest floor shimmer
                and break. I see the dead
        weave through maples.

                Alone with P.J. Harvey
                    cranked so loud it shakes the houses
            on Pearl Street—my mother playing cards
            at the bar until dawn, the neighbors
            staring at their ceilings but allowing it—

I repeat: *phalanges, mandible, ilium, scapula, scapula,*
                scrawling note cards for AP Bio.

After the divorce, my mother and I move
        from an 80-acre farm
    to a small house in town. She
    buys me nice curtains—lace, silk,
        blooming roses. But there is
    a strange man's voice upstairs.

            I vow: *No boy will ever touch me.*

Do we learn *phylum, rhombus, haiku* because of love
        or do we love each thing after learning it?

I sometimes kiss my books, sleep with them all around me, under the
pillow, beneath the sheets, paperbacks clutched to my chest like the stuffed
animals that flew from the back of a pickup, wheeled to bits
on the expressway and

                my father wakes up
            in the mountains without me
            or a combine's drone.

     *

Because we call our religion The Game, cut up
        my mom's nylons to make our doll-gods' robes.
My stepfather burns our spells, but the scriptures
        remain as squirrel skulls by the creek.
Because my best friend lets me sleep in her bed, steal
the blankets, and eat her Halloween candy,
        I put the gun back in my lunchbox; I read
Nietzsche from a Bible's leather case, and laugh it off
when at church camp, I'm pushed onto the stage.
      We un-baptize ourselves in the creek at 2 a.m. We ditch
        our cartoon pajamas.

     *

Because to impress my grandma, my grandpa turns his hat
         backwards and hurdles a four-foot gate.
   After her death, her porcelain angels gather a decade of dust, but
      he won't let us touch them.

Because The Unloved are nightly infused with radioactive brightness.
   Their parents hover around them
like desperate moths. No one remembers when the Un-Loved left
      or to where. Truths learned at cemeteries:
         1. If lightning had soft edges, it would resemble the soul.
         2. There is a soul.
         3. Souls hang out and fall in love, and there's nothing
            we can do to stop them.

Because I was afraid of the inside-dark but not the outside-dark, and the stars
were particularly talkative. They told me that time is hands
         rising to conduct a fugue.

Because all I've ever had, will have, imagined, spoken
      into the air, eyelashes blown from fingers, strands of hair
   stuck to the shower wall, petals ripped, meditations to expel desire,
   a Ken doll's torn leather jacket—rests on the beloved's worm-spun head.

GRACE

The old man huffs into his hands   *Our father,*
which art in heaven   from the print,
"Grace," while I march ponies
along my grandmother's shag carpeting.
He angles   *Hallowed be thy name*
free of the frame, placing me and my cousin
on the bed. We hold hands like always.

Thy kingdom come   Our pink
bodies are stripped and *Thy will be done*
he takes my cousin first,
biting her shoulder. *In earth*
Her baguette-limbs *In heaven*
steam into the old man's face. At five years old,
I have a nervous breakdown after seeing
a photo of my cousin. Her head is tilted to the right,
Our daily bread   and I can only see
one of her ears. I think the old man bit it off,
hear him heaving from the living room.
Thine is the kingdom   I shout,
"Her ear, her ear!" until the two words became *hear.*

My grandfather raped a twelve-year-old girl.
The power   He did the same
to my mother and uncle. *The glory*   Hear
the swish of pajamas on the stairs,
For ever and ever   dollars folded into pockets,
footfalls on a prison's linoleum,
pigeons mistaken for angels *Amen*
                    along a barbwire fence.

FIRST FATHER

Double fathers with double faces sing,
    a parallelogram of mouths rewrite
the silence: *night so long when time goes crawling.*
      They croon out discord, fight
    the static hum of feet—the desire to run.
He swung me through the air. The wind through
      my cells spun a web. O father, once
    I was a house collapsed, the blue
    silk I struggled to escape. Hank Williams,
      guitar in hand, lips open, knows
    a rambling man is only free in dreams.
    Behold each one—scarred, broken-nosed;
I've loved him. A killer in waves, I break
      and lift them like Achilles in your wake.

I WON'T REMEMBER

In every atom pulled with fingers careful
      of decay, I find your half-mooned eye.
  Down the windmill of cells, through air
and noise, embedded with Samurai
      grace, I dredge up respect—descant
of crows. What are you? A doll
  without a falcon cry, a sycophant
      whose tongue is sliced receipts? A toll
of discord sounds from your heart—the blue
  sky. Father, I've named you every star
      I see. Nebulas shriek their maxim—truth
is in forgetting. So I will. Bars,
  neglect, lies, forgotten. You're a sore
      with no platelets, an Olympic torch.

I'M AN APPARITION

You texted me, *Good Morning.* Shocked,
    I pictured you among Wyoming hills
and smiled to think of edges. We haven't talked
    in years. Miss you? And wish the snow-filled
yard a track, or the autumn leaves descend
        from branches all at once? You are what you are.
Those bagpipes wailing loud enough to summon
    up the dead can't call you home. Bizarre,
you wear destruction like a crown of laurel.
    Apollo of the Rockies—condescend
        to check your cell. I texted back, *Hello.*
I meant to say: Don't worry about the end
    or those you left. We don't matter. Just
        love the empty sky that conjures us.

HUSH

Little baby, Father cocks a forty-
    five one-handed. The blue expanse
        is shattered by a gunshot. I only
    want to play outside. There's still a chance
he'll shoot the cats from kitchen windows, so I
    wait with the hose. I'm tired of chasing
        the things I love to safety. Goodbye.
    There is a bee in your path I long for. Waiting
for the safety of the night, I dream the birds
    you shot for sport and wish their death masks
        struck in you a horror that was earthed
    long ago, when your old dog snapped
        at your father, and saying, *This is for the best*,
the old man shot him fourteen times, ploughed the carcass.

HANDS LIKE WRECKING BALLS

He takes the piston off the line,
    hoists it, lifts. He takes the piston
        off the line, vomits while
at work, hates his work. He is
    a plaid of wires, photons, bosons.
Father is a flannel blitzed
    with grass, a motor dodging
        lilies all around. He worships
friend-machines, but I've been knit
    with petals hammered to the barn.
He used to tuck his thumbs in his fists
    before he learned to punch with hands
        like wrecking balls, and once he beat
a boy almost to death for me.

FATHER TEACHES ME HOW TO KILL A MAN

We practice like dancers.
      Then he gives me a knife, says:

Cut upwards.
      But what about Mark,

sixteen, leaning over
      for a kiss on prom night—

his black suit, parents with careers? I
      clutch the knife's leather case

within my purse, push
      his face away with the other hand.

He cries, a thing
      I don't know boys can do.

Dave, Tony, Brent, Mark, Kevin—
      This is my apology: a slow dance,

a thousand drives with the windows down,
      birthday cards, love notes,

my two hands, a blade's
      soft rising in my throat.

AUBADE

You blacked out
    the night, forgot how we
jumped off cliffs into Lake Superior,
    the October water filling
    our mouths until we felt
    the gods get drunk
inside us. I long for you, the sun
    you turn toward me
    and away from me at will.
You're something I
    evaporate into, the way
    the water of our cells turns
    to rain when left
    outside. You forgot
    the origami snakes we lit, talking
    of Prometheus, his fire,
    the eagle that eats
his liver each morning. I spoke
    into the 4 a.m. darkness
    these things never happened,
    twisted your skin
    until it bruised, your moan
    an elegy to the last
    fluttering thing in my chest.
    Teach me to forget, to button
    sun over my breasts, explode
    my past in a nova
    of amniotic light. I swear,
    the storm took

your body, and through
 light flickering on our wet
shoulders, I learned
your consciousness hides
 in the undertow, can be tempted
 back with a single note
 from a longneck bottle.
 The wind had sounded that same
 low G through white pines
 for thousands of years.

HERO

All words collapse.
Calypso. Sun. A garden
weaving. I invoke
him: Cloud glove. Tree foot.
Blue grave. If he—
she—is a red bird's neck,
then I am betrayed.

I am a grave,
betrayed cloud,
the sunny garden-
blue Calypso
weaver of his collapsed neck.
Red bird: If
I invoke words—
a tree, glove, foot—
she is all.

She's Calypso,
but he's a cloud,
and I'm a red bird's neck.
If invoked, he betrays
because all words weave
graves: tree, glove,
sun, feet, blue, tree,
a garden collapsed.

DREAM OF ADAM

you drip mahogany and scarlet   vermillion
and blue   a riddle flung through caps
of honeycomb   gathering fistfuls of numbers
from your belly   open   waiting   for   a
place where ink   stretches   like palms
you bite into   a pineapple   cover the light
that spurts from your jugular   whisper
phyllotaxy and polygons absolute zero   it's good
so I hold your face   to my breast   which has not
yet rivered red clay from milk   *o snow crystal*
octahedron   you're my cloud's shut eye   the void
inside my childless   now the blue is static
and when we look inside each other   the root
of all evil   *infinitesimal*   comparison

III. POSSESSED GIRLS

Darkling I listen . . .
—John Keats, "Ode to a Nightingale"

PRAYER FOR DEAD BIRDS

I'm a green eye opening
        in the dark
of a laurel's insides,
    branches slipping
to a crown. I'm a stone pit,
        word-torch, coal-ink,
fiery mass of gristle.

O blown glass fallopian
        tubes, charred bits
    mixed with turkey bones:
they were wrong to cross us
with lighter fluid and flick
        a match. I'm the inside
of the inside of an egg,
    a clipped swallow's beak,
    the nest of pink birds
the cat ate, the leftovers
    waiting in a heap for dogs.

THE SHADOW OF MY BLACK DRESS

"And when you look long into an abyss,
the abyss also looks into you."
—Nietzsche, *Beyond Good & Evil*

You always go for a drive after
an episode, headlights God's bright
          gaze through parting
clouds. In the backyard
for luck, I catch bits of red
          from balding maples. There are
plenty of real ghosts
          on Pearl Street, but you
run from the shadow
     of my black dress hung to dry.
               The spirits here
                    mouth animal static
          from the bathroom mirror. I grow
into a reflection of myself that is
not myself, cast fishnets into shark-
          infested skies. Starlight, of course
we die alone. I just want someone
     to eat with me in the high school
cafeteria, but ghosts whisper
               in trochees. *Crazy*
          echoes from the first bottle
of Hot Damn I threw up as a child.
I'll travel back in time, Mother,
          hold your hand when
               the giant lobster hovers

over your bed, clicking its pincers.
But I'm not sorry. I wore your wedding dress
to a séance, which was not really
        speaking with the dead, but dancing
on your antique table. I haven't slept since you
        called an exorcist for me. Just
so you know: if that man you brought
        home from the bar takes
off his hat, I'll load my rifle. And Angel
        of Death: blow me.

MY BEST FRIEND AND ME

At ten, too old
 for dolls, we hide them.
The toy bin snaps
 like a sacred book's
binding. While our parents
 sleep, we write ourselves
 gods, and the simple plot
 we began spins from us until
the characters start
 to question the rules of
 their universe; they do
 terrible things; they horrify
and excite us until morning.
 And I wish I
 could end here, but the dolls
 are already changing faces,
appearing in drawers. My mother's
 car doors are opening
 by themselves, and the house
 is cold, cold
as the halls between biology
 and gym. We fail
 our classes. Someone yells
 lesbians; the word spits
like the fire pit where
 my stepfather burns
 dolls, poems, stories thick
 with dialogue. He calls
the exorcist, whose business card

was given to him by Pentecostal
ministers. These same men
 guide me through
a twelve-step recovery program
 for the possessed. I renounce
yoga. My parents
 divorce, and we move
 to another town. My little cousin
dies, but I dream it first.

TO CORA GOLDMAN, MY EXORCIST

In the woods behind
    my junior high, I hear
the first voice ringing through
      my bell-brain. I skip
    school in the rain, alone,
stare at the names scratched into
      an old shack. I hear
    the faintest answer to
      my questions: What is
    this place?

      Displaced. Why
am I here? *Mirror.*

      My hand won't go through
        the walls, and I
    push my voice so far
away I can speak to Kurt Cobain.

     *

The song inside my head:

    O holy nest, O halo net
      of Barbies,
heretic meteor hope
      for swing sets.

Crack the gibbous sky, crackers in the yard
            shooting birds from sun-baked
ditches, dust that brackets
        the pleading grackles,

        phantoms surging
            from rock, frothy rabid
dogs at my throat, jinxed tree-
            gutted filthy firmament.

Help me search the thunder for clean hands.

                    *

                You say:

Possessed girls have brown hair and hazel eyes.

Possessed girls channel demons to write poems.

Let your father stand behind you.

The witch's book always returns to her.

                    *

Broken bottle aimed at the refrigerator, I summon Joan
of Arc, my grandmothers, too-young brides counting

abortions on their fingers. I scrape my wrists each
night with my stepfather's
                    hunting knife. I hide
        under the kitchen table from
    the sound of fluttering. Azaleas
from my mother's garden desire the apocalypse:
        Breathe now tectonic
                    plates, jolt free the
            sod-wings latched to your backs.

                        *

Jesus-conjurer, girl-crusher, hummingbird vest,
        Leviathan: You're the pond
riddled with monsters. Hair feathered and lavender
        scented: the glaucoma sky.
                Dust-breather, beauty-eater:
            don't drag me from the hammock where I
                fan myself with hymnals. Don't draw
    oil crosses on my head.

                        *

Everyone is afraid of me.
                I rebuke thee.
Crossed with oil and ash
            In the name of Jesus
I'm thrown backwards

I rebuke thee.
Into my father's arms.
 In the name of Jesus
You say, they won't go.
   I rebuke thee.
Cora, do you want to know why
 In the name of Jesus
they won't go?
   I rebuke thee.
I'm the eye-full thing,
 the insect-thing, thorax,
venom, mandible, web.

POST-EXORCISM LUNCHROOM FUGUE

It's the sea of students parting for me. They hold
    their crosses, but it's too late. The gold
has eaten all the branches from their halos.

> *We live inside the air. We're folded*
> *dark matter, W.I.M.P.S.*
> *We move through you undetected.*

It's my head crossing into metal, my head lost
    in the living room where a cat tosses
its body into sunlit glass.

> *We live inside birds. We're mammoths buried*
> *under basements, glaciers.*
> *We move through you undetected.*

It's the scribbles on my face before school,
    the eye-shaped bruise
on my chest, the oil crosses Cora drew

on the mirror, banishing me from the trapeze
    world. It's nowhere to eat my string cheese.

POEMS BURNT IN A TRASH PIT

Along with my Manson, White Zombie, journals
of dialogue, her shredded white dresses.

Phrases drift from the fire:

                  darkness fades

egg of   jade.   Eros

    church bells

But it's my skin, my hair, my eyes burning.

              I saw Satan like lightning falling from heaven.

In the projected lung-chandelier
of my dreams, holograms flicker—

silhouettes of my sisters,
my not-sisters: daughters

of ink and lyre, metal-workers
bright with their own sparks.

I signed my poems *Eros,* and
they couldn't drag him from me with ash,

oil, fire, water, or verses.
He sleeps in black river stones.

The fifth horseman, vines stream from his back
as he roots the coffins, petioles the kneecaps.

Mother feels spring: Eros' egg in Eros'
darkness. She's a lighthouse with long black hair,

sea foam from Zeus' electric machete, and all
the planetary rings freeze in her yellow

wood-ringed iris. But Jehovah crumbles
her lighthouse with his fist. He bends

her machete into a wedding ring. He molds
her waves into a woman with a coal throat.

> *For Satan himself is transformed*
> *into an angel of light.*

I wake to a chorus
of revving engines.

Jehovah says, *Her blood cries*
to me. Seven coins times

ten murdered girls equals
the radioactive skull

where I bury eggs. Splinter and sing
for what is unseen: albino, holy, winged.

In Death's temple, I paint her
sleeping and awake—Eve (Eternal

Mother) equals an ash-dappled breast,
a broken macaroni necklace.

Thou shalt not suffer a witch to live.

Now Mother is afraid of the sky,
the clouds' violet violence and lie

of spring, grafts that don't flower
true from seed, faces lingering

in the cold, chaos-spun, pink sucker-
punch. First she will fear

water, then heights, the blue
itself a crumpled breathe-bag.

And I saw a new heaven and a new earth:
for the first heaven and the first earth
were passed away; and there was no more sea.

Mother sings me to sleep, and the prisms
above my bed sing with her,

but she sees shadows where I see beauty,
and she would burn me, shave my head and drag me

down Main Street for Jehovah, and I would let her
just to watch the stones call out from the courthouse:

Eros   Eros Eros

Oil from the gas tanks:

        Eros   Eros

Eros

Her secret name and my secret name asbestos
in the lungs of every passerby.

> *And I saw three unclean spirits like frogs*
> *come out of the mouth of the dragon,*
> *and out of the mouth of the beast, and out of the mouth*
> *of the false prophet.*

I call my mother:

—What made you think I was possessed?

—That woman was awful.

—Cora. What made you think I was possessed?

—I was afraid of her.

—She would sit at the St. Johns Big Boy, watching me. What made you think I was possessed?

—There's nothing wrong with you.

—I'm writing about the exorcism, the burning.

—Do what you have to do to survive.

Fly letters. Fly ink. Fly
trees from the paper. Fly
Jesus. Fly bonfire. Little poems, fly.

DRIVING HOME FROM CHOIR PRACTICE

I crashed my Grand Am into a ghost,
got out of the car and searched the tall grass.
I saw his blue eyes first.

> *Andromeda, o cricket*
> *Anthropomorphic thicket*
> *Throats of morphing birds*

I dialed my best
friend, then breathed into a plastic bag.
I crashed my Grand Am into a ghost

> *Hominids crawl*
> *Trailer halls*
> *Walls inherit holes*

a year after I prophesized my cousin's encephalitis
as a flood drowning him in his crib.
I saw his blue eyes first.

> *Lazuli serpent*
> *Lazarus spent*
> *His eyes persist*

Mother doesn't believe in psychiatrists,
only demons, so I can't confess:
I crashed my Grand Am into a ghost,

Car doors open
Carrion doors
Without hands

and I need my fucking head checked. I crossed
my photos with oil when
I saw his blue eyes—

Armor of God
Amorous God
A morose God

the first step to getting rid of spirits.
My aunt wouldn't let me in her house after
I crashed my Grand Am into a ghost.
First, eye blue his saw I:

Air, o grant
Aerial graves
To my enemies

SONG OF THE COCKROACH ANGEL

Before I met Cora, I dreamed
that my dead siblings grew like cucumbers
in a field. As I wandered towards
the tree of life, frogs perched on the blurry flap
of skin between my legs. Now,
instead of the otherworld, there is a baseball diamond.
Over the PA, she chants:
Forget time's rings—dance in Rubik's
cubes. Crow the tree's knobby breasts.
She pitches a fastball; the crowd boos.
Aleph, the gray sky. Aleph, the sea-
green fugue. Release your enemies.
I've got a crew cut; my chest is the flat, white
pearl in her gut.
Go back to the field. There's a string
to cut: a bell a body rings.

IV. LILY AND GOG

I fell back in love with you, Father, for two reasons:
You were good to me, & a delicious author,
rational & passionate. Come on me again,
as you twice came to Azarias and Misael.
—John Berryman, "Eleven Addresses to the Lord"

LILY AND GOG

The Sacred Pool

The field where I was raped was once
a sacred pool. Crows ate holy raspberries,
which Lily planted and cared for,

a river nymph with long blue hair.
I could speak to the earth after Chris
dragged me through a field. I screamed

Golden Goddess of the Corn! and became the stalks'
rustling, leaves, gravel, swallows, pheasants.
I transformed myself at the slightest suffering.

Lily cried into the pool for her stolen daughter,
Gog, slashed her breasts and wrists, sang
lavender spikes through the water.

In her grief, she welded her body
to the bedrock like a petrified trout.
Gog would turn into a monster,

the biblical harbinger of the apocalypse,
but we didn't know that yet. The dirt
scrambled my voice into a harpsichord's

arpeggios. Lily woke from a thousand
years of sleep, then quicksilvered
into my body. It rained

as I sifted home. For days,
I stared at the basketball hoop. Cages
and nets have little matter, mostly space.

Heathen in Fishnets

Birds liked to watch us, me and Lily, blast
constellation-hymns at trees, refusing
to mow the lawn or wash dishes.

Lily mummified herself with the coils
of my Disney tapes, tied my dolls
to jump ropes and smashed their faces.

If I were Snow White, barn swallows
would hang laundry on the line, suds beef
off floral plates. Lily moved like paint rinsed

from a brush, smearing the soybeans' edges.
Band practice was a joke as she pulled
the silver of my flute into ropes, wrapping

percussionists in metallic halos. Mr. Krauss
could not conduct without her blowing
in his ear. The lunchroom was a chaos.

I watched from the courtyard, a Goth,
heathen in fishnets, head adorned
with sticky black diamonds. Inside my chest,

pythons writhed and languished
at the sight of Jeff, same name as my father.
His thin, white skin glowed in the spaces

between tattoos. His Manson shirt
read: *No Forgiveness. No Mercy.* I wondered,
had Jeff read Nietzsche's *Antichrist*?

Was his Hyperborean tongue
as blue as a corpse's? Would he bind
my heart in pine or plastic?

The UFO

We liked to go camping,
me, Liisa, and Lily. In the field
behind my farmhouse, we learned

imagination is a kind of death, a wilderness
of the collective's manic fits. There is one story,
and it opens like a music box.

The ballerina's legs are worn of ligaments.
She turns with a screech. We saw a UFO,
and after, form and shadow didn't match.

We lined our doll's eyes with ink,
cut off the crowns of their heads,
then watched their faces change.

We both saw them: the dark-winged creatures
we had no name for, spinning
like planets as we played.

Cora the Exorcist

Cora burned my *Antichrist*s, the Manson album
and the text, along with my poems and journals.
They thought I was possessed, and I was.

Sometimes Cain winged around my bed
while Lily's lightning flickered like a bug zapper.
Sometimes Cora gripped

my shoulders and shouted, "In the name of Jesus!"
And I wished Jesus possessed so many colors,
although I loved to kiss his pale stone lips

above the altar while my grandmother,
church secretary, wrote the newsletter.
Christ understood to suffer

is an explosion of pink, Alice falling
down the tree. And beauty, luminous,
is the thing that feeds her wandering.

Lily wanted to burn him on a pyre.
Lily wanted to lie in a hammock.
Lily wanted to honor him with fire.

February Exorcism

Cora checked me for demons
on Saturdays at the St. Johns Big Boy.
While I waited tables, I learned

to push Lily into the sky. February exorcism:
Cora knocked at our door. I had just
coated my legs with cucumber lotion. She was armed

with a Bible, holy water, ash
and extra virgin olive oil. I put my biology
notes away. I dressed like a sacrifice—

curled hair and pink fingernails.
Our dog barked and ran in circles.
Cora held me still, and I could smell

the Aqua Net in her towering bangs.
She gripped my shoulders. My father stood behind
in case I tried to run. My mother and uncle

stood at my flanks. They were terrified,
and my laughing slashed time's fabric.
I saw men in funny hats, deer

shot with arrows. She cast out
the characters from my stories—
Jacob, Vivian, Cain, Shalloch!

I couldn't stop laughing, saw the aurora
borealis, the dream where I was flying,
and I begged the gods to turn me into a nebula

where stars are born. And I breathed
like a flame, deep inside a supernova,
exploded into dust, Saturn's rings.

Cora said, *There is one*
demon left! And she wrapped Jesus' name
all around. *One left!* Lily, asleep in the garden.

Gog Returns

Lily heard Gog singing in the night's arrow.
Gog sang like a lowing cow, lost daughter,
in love with her plate of sorrow.

Gog! Gog! And she didn't answer. So Lily
chased her: down Pearl Street,
past the Ovid Bar, East Street Cemetery,

under the creek, across doe's tongues
through racks of bucks, above
the Walmart Superstore, past abandoned

Main Street, Lansing's gray
capital, Sparty's underwear,
then deep into the undertow of Lake

Superior, north to Canada, Hudson
Bay, the snow of the Arctic,
by the fur of seals, weaving

through the goddess, Tiamat's, squid-ink hair
and sinking, finally, in a bed of shipwrecks,
at the center of a glacier.

Gog whispered to her billions of irises.
She was gifted with an eyeball for each
extinct species. From each eye

sprang a phantom. Each phantom cradled
one million years of history—
pterodactyls, slugs, and wooly mammoths roiled

in bright spheres. A brontosaurus'
roar made Lily jump. She was wind
halting, suddenly, in a forest.

Dearest Gog, she began, *my lost daughter,*
my raspberry, first bud, sun-behind-
my-thumb—you're the red of the blackbird's

wing, the pink of crabapples. Rising,
Gog replied: *The world calls me*
Medea, Lilith, Demon of the Deep.

I taste "mother" in my mouth, a blowfish
barbed and swollen. Love, after fighting
a thousand wars, killing countless infants

as they dreamt of shell-wombs, bundled
in their mothers' arms? My children laugh
at suffering, outside of time, immortal.

What are you to me now, lowly pond-
nymph? I could crush you in an instant.
You, of tears and green, dare descend

to monochrome eternity? With this,
Gog trapped Lily in an orb
of blue, prismatic, swirling ice.

Lily the Stag

Bailing hay, in Michigan, a chill spread
like roots. I took off my flannel shirt
and swung from the hay loft, walked

past tractor engines, the ladies lace
I liked to pick and twirl, the picnic table
where my grandma sat pitting cherries,

hopped in my Grand Am and drove
to Pearl Street in an iron trance. My mother,
newly divorced, would not be home

until morning. The mums rose
to meet the sun, the leaves upturned
their palms. I prayed: *Dearest Lord, rainbow-*

in-the-oil-slick, ant-warrior-thorax:
Get me out of this town.
I fell asleep, and in my dream,

Lily spoke as a stag, showed me
the trees' buzzing
breath, beyond visible light.

The Dream

Leaves were glazed with silver; beams of red,
orange, blue, green, and white
flooded skyward. Our souls cometed

through a fifth dimension, teeming
with images from our past incarnations.
Lily's antlers were electricity,

her coat speckled with stars. I knelt
and touched my nose to her muzzle,
and her song pierced my being:

Corn-daughter, fight, warrior flight, as primordial
darkness was one with the light, so shall you wear
the weavers' web of cobalt.

She sank the glowing blue armor
into my skin, and like a black rose,
I bloomed into the night. Lily's next words

filled the whole forest: *Corn-daughter, wake!*
Then I woke to hear my own mother spill
her purse onto the floor, three in the morning, home

from the bar. She tucked the sheets
around my shoulders, kissed my head.
I wrote a lullaby, tried to remember it

as I drifted, saw a figure fly, Gog's litter
approached, and I began to hum.
I woke to see my mother sitting

beside me; she held my hand. I woke
alone in a field of infants, umbilical
cords attached like vines. I woke

inside a flaming oak and felt my lips
harden into bark. Gog and her children wailed
a dissonant fugue, hissed

my name. I saw the intricate whorls
of their throats, the way they tenderly grazed
their bodies against one another. Gog hurled

Lily, now an icy prism, into my eyes.
Fragments protruded from my face—
an antler, Lily's Tree of Life

a broken crystal toy. The weaver's
web-armor began to throb and I felt
the stirring of my spinnerets, more

eyes bloomed from my cheeks. I cracked
the tree and rose, First Woman, silk
gland, ovary, book lung, neck,

shoulder, thorax, leg, and egg sack.
I swallowed the prism, and with each bite
the orchestral passion of Lily's song burst

from my hybrid body. And Gog's children
began to dance! Gog cackled,
untying her robe. She let it drop, and radiant

spiders spiraled through her as she transformed herself—
an archangel, Hera, Kurt Cobain, Jesus, a crone, a stag.
As she picked a blue spider from her horns,

I flung my body from the flames, singing
Lily's music, then "Jesus Don't Want Me
for a Sunbeam," "All Apologies"

the words flowering through us, and somehow,
Gog loved to hear her mother, safely dead,
through another's puppet-mouth.

Gog wrapped me in her silk. We swelled to a cocoon,
but I hatched alone, the dryer clinking, coffee brewing.
Sunlight sparked behind the curtains.

LOVE POEM TO THE LIGHT BEFORE SLEEP

These, my lips, parted with an oh-
    hell-oh-man. Pale angel's
        bag of suns, my heart counts new
mornings by a face held to my belly. A great orb

    silvers over the magnetic coil
of my sex tapes—oh, various enlightenments
        swell and crush, but
you are atomic, killer, my darling

    dear of the capsized raiment—
    there are seven deadly sins I'd sickle
onto my soul for one brush of your stubbly
        chin against my cheek

because this, my voice,
    sounds as sand in the night's
 eyeball, where I wrap
      my legs like a vine

    and I have known
     the heart of the earth. Never sun
     because fire gets pissed into nebulas—
but not you, great atrium, Picasso

 nose, purple vortex of my dreams,
    the star-field I duck through
while wooing this, my air, my open
      birdcage of breath.

WAITING FOR THE RESULTS

I'm lava in a box of ashes. O
skin! Rain down on me in puddles

I used to skip through, like matter,
like I matter on this earth.

Call me in the summer—
blistered, childless, alone. I'll say

I love it all. And I'll be a liar. Open
the box. Go ahead. Worms will fly

into your face, and you'll smile.
The sky won't answer me, but shoots

through my back with its poison
arrows. You shouldn't have touched

my lip with your thumb.
Then I wouldn't be dying. I wouldn't know

the things we love are luminous,
wings beating like a storm-whipped flag.

*

I blew this town after the bark fell off
the only oak that hadn't been hewn. Brutal
Father blows programs from the pulpit,

wrenches open my soul-flask
of Hennessey. You know me,
Lord. I'm the one wearing

dirty underwear, creeping
from my boyfriend's with haystack
hair. I'm ready for

annihilation. I get it—
sparks of quanta, the collage
of bones in a speck of dirt—

life is beyond
sacred. Each of us contains
the spark of creation, so it makes me

crazy: Ebola, the Holocaust, dead soldiers
in a field. I'm ready
for angels to trumpet inside me,

waking everything that lived until
this world is a
junkyard of skulls.

JOHN KEATS!!

Keats flowers above
 my bed like drops of blood
in dishwater. Queen of
 shadows, negative capability is a dragon

 blown into twenty thousand years
of sea foam, distant green gardens. My dark star's
X-rays show bright, steadfast—
 six fingers, six toes. Tender is the night.

This doesn't mean oceans turn to acid
 or billboards eclipse the sun. In those ceaseless shadows
nothing will die except old chargers, unchangeable
 priestlike rotary phones, desktop computers.

 Mother told me I was afraid
 of the circle
 hovering around me as I slept, but I don't remember
 anything except how I
 climbed into bed
with her, wishing
 I were a ballerina
 sinking too fast, the world a gash of paint.

Printers, fax machines, books—they remember
 an asylum of nightingales. They grow faces.

*

Your eyes are a thing I would worship, Collective Ghost,
eating crackers and milk for dinner, hours

before the TV oracle, our bodies
        locked tight as remote controls against the night.

If we could stop loitering in the valley
of immortal birds, embalmed, haunted: *Darkling, listen,*
        I was running late and
                forgot to pack your lunch.

Keats surges
        through eyes of mounted bucks
on the walls of the room where
        I hide under comforters (hide with me).

*

This is a requiem for those who have crossed the valley
of leptons, believing in telescopes, microscopes, horoscopes.

This is a requiem for those who have wandered the Atlanta airport
looking for a place to charge their Androids.

This is a requiem for the barista at Starbucks;
she conjures the vale of smile-making to hide her hate,

for me and everyone, which I ball up like a terrible report on giraffes.
In my childhood, there were four dreams:

Covered in snakes, Mother reads
by a lake of fire.

Old Man bites
my shoulders.

Farmhouse falls
into the cracked ground.

The porcelain cowgirl begins breathing
so I strangle her.

*

Remember those who have crossed: shapes without bells,
glades of form paralyzed.

Dear Nightingale, Pale Fingernail of the Moon,
the air above your bed teems with ribbons

that undulate through you. This is the nature of the self!
Preserve her anthem.

We sail
through winking universes, write
our names on each other's backs.
Keats's wings—tidal waves, cellophane—scrape

against peeling wallpaper,
      while we conjure all the promises
our mothers didn't keep.

    *

This is the Porcupine Mountains, the Communist Manifesto of light
reflected on a leaf's veined belly, infinitesimal calculus with stabs
of ice. If your being prays like a foot pressed
to a thousand crystal jellyfish—

                  I hiked eight miles and
          didn't bring any water, high enough to kiss
             with parted lips.

The children won't stop eating Lethe-blueberries, my purple-stained
mouth fades into the forest, my dim heart aches. Think
about how sick I'd get if I drank from those magic
eternal lids, that lake of fire.

Far away, dissolved in a fever of hemlocks,
groan gray specters, jay-eyed despairs. To float between
dendrites, let's play the sky's helium mistress.

Waking alone, all softness falls and swells,

I hear an immortal bird like a flute
in this valley of organic trail mix.

Swell shells singing *Fair creature of an hour!* What if you showed us
Death and we could feel it? Far away, an anthem:
Dissolve the fever and groan-gray-specter-eyed despair.

    *

How have we been living
with this purple eye, flashlight, orb
of rooftop cigarettes, kernels sprouting under snow?

Between the neutrino and the proton,
between the meteor and the tree,
the 92 elements. We sail through
       winking universes, write
our names on each other's backs.
  Our wings—tidal waves, cellophane—scrape,
          while Keats conjures all the promises
        his mother didn't keep. Soft fallen splendor masks

the robin and the egg. Rosy hues download and bless

the dinosaur and the robin fair—
the eleventh dimension of sawdust.

    *

        Another dream where Keats leads
          me through his childhood home.

There's a stone door in back of
an apothecary room.

No one is around. Except us. Beyond
the door there is an ancient, flooded forest.
We swim through leaves. Clouds are
also underwater, and

Gates open from sun-sparks, while

Each tree groans. *Here* (where bees are seahorses)

Lies one whose name was writ . . .

*

I dipped the pennies in ketchup,
then coke. They got so clean I reinvented
1971. Now my mother is nine, the casements of her
purple-stained mouth fade in the forest dim.
      I told the little girl my mother almost adopted,
      You can't see darkness with your eyes shut.
        But I had no advice for the bathtub, where
her mother had held her under.

Does your heart ache? Are hemlocks the trees of our foam? Me and you.
Us floating, o faery power, o those who have crossed,
cells of requiem sod, soft-lifted and winnowing
immortal birds, ancient clown-swath and twined flowers.

In a stuffed kingdom, spiral vines, cheese sandwiches
in the shape of Elvis, Reader, they say the most beautiful words are:
cellar door. I have none, and you are dreaming (cellar door)
of all the souls yet to be born.

*

Keats's readers wink around him: millions of fire-eyes,
wounds of purple fire wide.

He is the photographed. He is the photographer.
He is the season of mists and mellow fruitfulness.

We are sparks of nothingness, pennies pennies pennies, yet
Chris pinned my arms to the grass. Fear were you?

On the grass where you have fallen asleep.

*

My dull brain repeats: Tender is.
The anti-night, queen-blown verdurous feet of dawn, furrowing,
embalmed eyes I will not meet in dreams.

I took a selfie to commemorate our

dark star, dark star, wailful,

singing treble in Death's green kingdom. To float between

dendrites, we play the sky's helium mistress. We wear nothing,
fuck in the language of moths. It's true: oozing inside

our entrails, the things-yet-to-be-born wink and flutter, while
barred clouds bloom patient, tender-taken. We swoon.

*

Death I see you. Death I hear you—
                Open the morning,
                    wait for hatchlings
        to crack open
        their mouths. Snakes spill out
into the field where you are my eyes and my mother—

Keats, melodious and green,
sings us an ode, full-throated, back to a deep-delved country
whose songs will flicker and swarm him, fume poppies
and hook him where he is sleeping in 1818,
numbing his arms and legs.

Keats has grown good
with his purple eye and mess of air
        soft on my pillow. He saws
                into my chest and eats the bandages.

*

Fair Creature of an Hour! Starbucks Barista!

I'll be Dante. You be Virgil.
    You be hell.
    I'll be your delicious icy core.

WHY THE WORKING CLASS WON'T SAVE US

"So Miss Fluke and the rest of you feminazis,
here's the deal. If we are going to pay for your contraceptives
and thus pay for you to have sex, we want something.
We want you to post the videos online so we can all watch."
—Rush Limbaugh

Giant Cow on Main Street, Deity of Broken Bottles,
Goddess of the Dollar Menu, you know a 6' tall
German-American wearing a Pantera t-shirt
called me a dyke, then spit in my face. When my stepfather's guru,
Rush Limbaugh, calls law student, Sandra Fluke, a "slut"
and a "prostitute," I think of corsets,
clitoridectomies, fusing the labia-wound,
the miracle-womb, fetus-fish feeding, the cervix
widening and the infant's brain-burst
into air. *Bitch, ice queen, feminazi.* Every woman
in my family has been raped. My belated protection:
petrifaction, the tree's innermost ring drained
of sap, black lipstick and necklace-dagger. My stepfather said,
eyes factory-dust red, oil-stained fingers:
"You're lucky. You're a girl so it doesn't matter
what you do with your life." He worked third shift
at Sealed Power on a steel ring assembly line, said: "I've read
two books—hated both." My grandma told my mom
she was a fool to divorce "the kind of man who puts food
on the table," and hell, I thought her a crazy old lady
until my mother brought home a lineup of abusers.
My mother: "There's no way around hellfire."
Confusion is the devil. Doubt, devil. Questions, devil.
Me, devil. I escaped the blond spitter,

made a doll of his likeness and stuck it with pins.
And no matter how many times I hollered at those farm boys
they tortured the newborn bulls.

But I met my true love by a river.
We couldn't see the river because we were really at a burger joint.
Yet a single eye opened beneath that muck, colored
like a monarch's wing. And the eye rose and with it, a face,
then breasts—Eva, Eva, my ancestress's corpse
lit up and I finally understood the way around hellfire
is a pure cleaving to the present, that I would kiss the Goliath
bird-eater tarantula's web of your frontal lobe. We painted
each other's faces like dragons, and the river's song
doesn't change, not even when it's toxic, littered
with plastic bottle caps and sludge. The soul cleaves.
Supernal lights wink through the branches, and I cling there,
listening to you read Mina Loy poems, the sun
half on my face, and we're cut from a chrysalis
like super-monarchs, like those goddamn
Nymphalidae flying to the high mountains of Mexico, miles
above the cities like airwaves, fearless,
prismatic with the strength of what we've learned.

I COULD PUT MY HAND THROUGH

Rothko's red   three-dimensional   blinded
by linear time   pull out my mother   bleeding
and fifteen   in the fourth dimension   each is
a snake   to make a thing breathe   it must balance
zygote head   corpse tail   heaven and psilocybin
by an invisible string   we aren't allowed to touch
only to see   until our eyes   are angels who crash
into the vaulted ceiling   we have no mass   god's
hair-field keeps   our atoms   from flying at
the speed of light   after the National Gallery
I want to burn   starting with my eyes

ELEVEN ELEVEN

In the gray temple, ashes snow around us.
Two pillars, phallic, supernal, Grandma's gray

face, her hair wrung into wet, straight points. She's young.
Her pregnant belly pulses like a speaker.

I jump awake: eleven eleven. My
grandfather keeps her remains in a cardboard box.

Someday I'll streak them across my face.
In numerology, eleven is the master number.

World War I ended on November eleventh,
at eleven. Of the 33 Vedic gods,

eleven dwell on earth, eleven in the heavens
and eleven in mid-air. The devil's

tongue; the cross turned in on itself; two fingers
to the lips; the number of years it takes me to

gain back my visions after my mother calls an exorcist.
Grandma dies after a year and a half

of radiation on 11/11/2001.
My torso plus my beloved's torso, two legs,

two arms entwined, the first gray snakes to create
the universe, two lines running parallel

for infinity. Berryman's "Eleven Addresses to the Lord,"
section 11, line 11: *Cancer, senility, mania . . .*

LESSONS IN SACRIFICE

Let's say you're a bridge operator   Mother lectures
you lift for ships   *lower for trains*   I'm the only one
in first grade   *when your son catches his coat*
in the gears   whose fingers form the Vulcan sign
for live long and prosper   *you must drop the bridge*
and crush him   so I make little spring bunnies
saving hundreds   by dipping my hands in paint
Mother says   *a Witness is chased by soldiers*
as self-punishment   for forgetting they symbolize
Easter   *there's a river   too wide to cross*   I walk
barefoot through thistles   *yet he says "Jehovah"*
stand in the dark basement for hours   *and leaps*
the clouds thunder   *whoever sins*
against Him   *will be erased from the book*

CULT OF THE DRYAD

Mother, mother, mother—say it until she
wakes inside a poplar, smear
her on shower walls. Dryad transforms
her globular soul into a bulls horn and
nostrils, ladder-vine of faces, code of
flickering light. Dryad reveals:

    Orpheus was man and woman.
        Double-souled. Sometimes, his bed head
surged like the wings of a blackbird.
        Snakes coiled in his hips and he prowled
the hills invoking Zeus. Or he wiped
        his lips with the back of his hand,
divine rage prisming through him
        at the sight of tree-knob breasts.
Imagine a garden without gates, water
        that is light, a place where grass speaks.

    *

Whenever I think of Orpheus, I
remember Mother's aerial
cartwheels. A man pushes her
into the fireplace. I'm born
red and armed with a BB gun. I aim
for his face. So why does Easter grass
float around my head? Why does Mother

shout as her boyfriend's minivan
rounds a corner? I'm born
inside my sister's grave. Mother's acrobat-
soul loops inward like
intestines. During a camping trip,
her father left her at the lake.
Why are some of us disposable?
My friend, Jenny, with the amber
hair, lifted up her shirt, and we
thumbed each cigarette scar.

                    *

Floodwaters rise like the part of the soul
that wanders after the mind
stops, that claws from spirit
to flesh, clings to brown
eyes, blue dress, green, red, child's
coiled fingers, child I abandoned.
So what if I spent
all night in Dryad's chest, was
burnt and burnt but refused to
die? Inside each trunk
a woman sleeps, and
within us, Dryad rages.
Trees can read our minds as
they sing. We mistake them
for angels, and amoebic
succubae creep into our homes
to torture us while we're
asleep. Dryad commands, say it:

I'll consume everyone I love,
    growing round, grass will
poke from my chin, and I'll make you
    remember what a woman is.

*

She's made of cellulite and
mountains, fell asleep 35,000
years ago. She's got the head
of a buffalo, and birthed
a trillion sea monsters. She's
split into plants, animals, insects,
colors, planets, electrons. She's a man
in the shell of sleep but a woman
when she eats her young, is rock
split by plate tectonics and
meteors. Philosopher's
brains are made of
her vagina. Hail! She'll tell you
what you like. Hail melting
on your face and hands, and fingers
reaching to tug her hair, river-long
with flames—Dryad sings:

    Daughters of the trees! Wash your scars
        in water made of light. Rise, dead sisters!
    Orpheus, man and woman, harvest
        ballads from the woods.
    Muses, drag your filthy, drag your knotted
        hair from graves and let us shave it.

TO BEAUTY

You are a child's
      marble face, glued
lips, thumb of twilight
at his throat, Blood—
 how the whole earth can fit
inside its color. Cut
flowers—cheerful snap of
limb from body. And
isn't grief a cold river,
      the bottom untouched by
a human foot? Create in me
      blue spruce, limestone.
Let me be mountains.
    I see the purple
phlegm of a ghost: my shut
      heart; my shut,
watery heart; the exorcist's
hands on my chest—her
 spinning crown; the caw
 of tires as my mother speeds
      away. Psalms, let
the ones you have crushed
 arc around my bed with wings
outstretched. Grandmother,
 imagine your daughter's
yellow eyes a demon's—your husband
who crept inside your daughter's
 dream-skin; a slick, silt-footed
nightmare—always a mirror's

breath from inside me; insects
impaled with pins; keys
buried in the ditch; phantoms
 with mouths like wilting
petals. Of all the gates
         to heaven, I choose
 an eye: Iris, unhinged; horses
tumbling through clouds as
I tumble through
         daylight. May it never
end, this feathered thing.

THE BEASTS THAT BEAR JEHOVAH

From the backyard maple, I drop
robin eggs onto the grass, peer
at the scarlet yokes, listen for the embryo's
imagined cry. Instead of memorizing
the books of the New Testament,
I gain ten pounds, making decisions
based on divination:
i.e. Should I eat a donut?
I flip open Job 1:20: *Then Job arose*
and rent his mantle, and
shaved his head, and fell down
upon the ground. The donut will
be chocolate. I set out a plate
of cheese for Gus each night,
the Cinderella-mouse my father shoots
while I'm at the Kingdom Hall. He leaves
the gun on the table. Since we don't
celebrate birthdays, my parents
declare a "Brandi Day." I run
through the aisles of Toys "R" Us, while
they wander hand-in-hand.
The heavenly beasts
that bear the divine light
on their backs can't see it. My mother
sings to her belly
as if it harbors a child.
They had joy. They had fun.

ACKNOWLEDGMENTS

First, I would like to thank my professors at Florida State University for their support during my MFA and PhD: David Kirby, Barbara Hamby, James Kimbrell, Erin Belieu, S.E. Gontarski, Eva Amsler, and Daniel Vitkus. When I arrived in 2008, I didn't know how to break a line. You helped me revise and re-envision these poems time and again. Thank you as well to FSU's very talented graduate students for your insightful comments. This book is certainly a collaborative effort. Additionally, I owe a great deal to my friends at Northern Michigan University. If not for the encouragement of Kevin Avery, Richard Berrigan, Ajani Burrell, Anthony Guerriero, Molly Guerriero, Jason Shrontz, Stacey TerBeek Shrontz, Eric Smith, Sarah Wangler, and Jennifer Yeatts, I wouldn't have had the courage to show anyone my poems in the first place. A huge thanks to NMU professors Beverly Matherne and Austin Hummell, who helped me with every poem in my MFA application, as well as Ray Ventre, who read me Whitman poems in his office. Thank you as well to Claudia Emerson, you are missed, Robert Hass, and the rest of my amazing workshop group at Sewanee Writer's Conference. Additionally, I would like to thank Hambidge Center for the Arts and Hill House Institute for Sustainable Living, Art & Natural Design for granting me the time and space to work on these poems. I wouldn't have grown nearly as much as a writer without my amazing, ever-evolving, poetry group: Sandra Simonds, Vincent Guerra, Josephine Yu, Erin Higgins, Tana Welch, Timothy Welch, Nick Sturm, and Carrie Lorig. I can't thank you enough. Also, Jennifer Schomburg Kanke, what would I do without the intelligence, perceptiveness, and sanity you offer at our weekly coffee dates? And to all the editors and staff at Black Lawrence Press, particularly Diane Goettel, thank you for bringing this book to life.

I'm especially grateful to Liisa Clapp for twenty-three years of love and friendship. Thank you as well to my mother, as always, we're in this together. And, of course, none of these poems would have been possible without my first and best reader, my husband, Michael Barach. May we always find each other.

Finally, I would like to thank the following journals, in which these poems first appeared:

Another Chicago Magazine: "Meadows Trailer Park, 1995"
Best New Poets 2010: "To Beauty"
Cimarron Review: "Her Mouth, a String-less Lyre"
Clackamas Literary Review: "John Keats!!"
Columbia Poetry Review: "Why the Working Class Won't Save Us"
Confrontation: "Father Teaches Me How to Kill a Man"
Connotation Press: "Love Manifesto," "Sunday Tractor Pull"
CutBank: "Mother's Red Wedding Dress"
DIAGRAM: "Hero"
Entasis: "Waiting for the Results," "Homunculus"
The Fiddlehead: "Elegy for Myself at Six"
Fugue: "Mother Is a Wolf"
Gulf Coast: "To Cora Goldman, My Exorcist," "Song of the Cockroach Angel"
Harpur Palate: "First Father," "I Won't Remember," "I'm an Apparition," "Hush," "Hands Like Wrecking Balls"
The Iowa Review: "Lessons in Sacrifice"
La Fovea: "Cult of the Dryad"
Mayday: "Love Poem to the Light Before Sleep"
New Poetry from the Midwest 2014: "My Best Friend and Me"
New South: "Aubade"
Ninth Letter: "Crone-Ballad"

Prairie Schooner: "My Best Friend and Me"

Salamander: "For Eva, Who I Am Not"

Steel Toe Review: "Poems Burnt in a Trash Pit," "Driving Home from Choir Practice," "Post-Exorcism Lunchroom Fugue"

Weave: "The Shadow of My Black Dress"

Zone 3: "Lily and Gog," "Grace"

Photo: Kira Derryberry

Brandi George grew up in rural Michigan. Poems from her first collection of poetry, *Gog* (Black Lawrence Press, 2015), appeared in *Gulf Coast, Prairie Schooner, Best New Poets 2010, Ninth Letter, Columbia Poetry Review,* and *The Iowa Review.* She has been awarded residencies at Hambidge Center for the Arts and the Hill House Institute for Sustainable Living, Art & Natural Design, and she attended the Sewanee Writer's Conference as a Tennessee Williams Scholar. She currently resides in Tallahassee, where she is a Kingsbury Fellow and PhD candidate at Florida State University.